Poems about SCHOOL

Compiled by Brian Moses Artwork by Kelly Waldek

Other titles in the series:

Poems about Animals
Poems about Food
Poems about Space

Editor: Sarah Doughty
Designer: Tessa Barwick

First published in 1999 by
Wayland Publishers Ltd
61 Western Road, Hove
East Sussex, BN3 1JD

Find Wayland on the Internet at http://www.wayland.co.uk

British Library Cataloguing in Publication Data
Poems about School – (Wayland poetry collections)
    1. Schools – Juvenile poetry   2. Children's poetry,
English
    I. Moses, Brian, 1950 –
821.9'14'08'0355

ISBN 0 7502 2439 8

Printed and bound by Edições ASA, Portugal

All Wayland books encourage children to read and help them improve their literacy.

✓ Themed poetry is ideal for use as part of the literacy hour.

✓ The page numbers and index of first lines can be used to find a particular poem.

✓ The books to read section suggests other books dealing with the same subject.

Contents

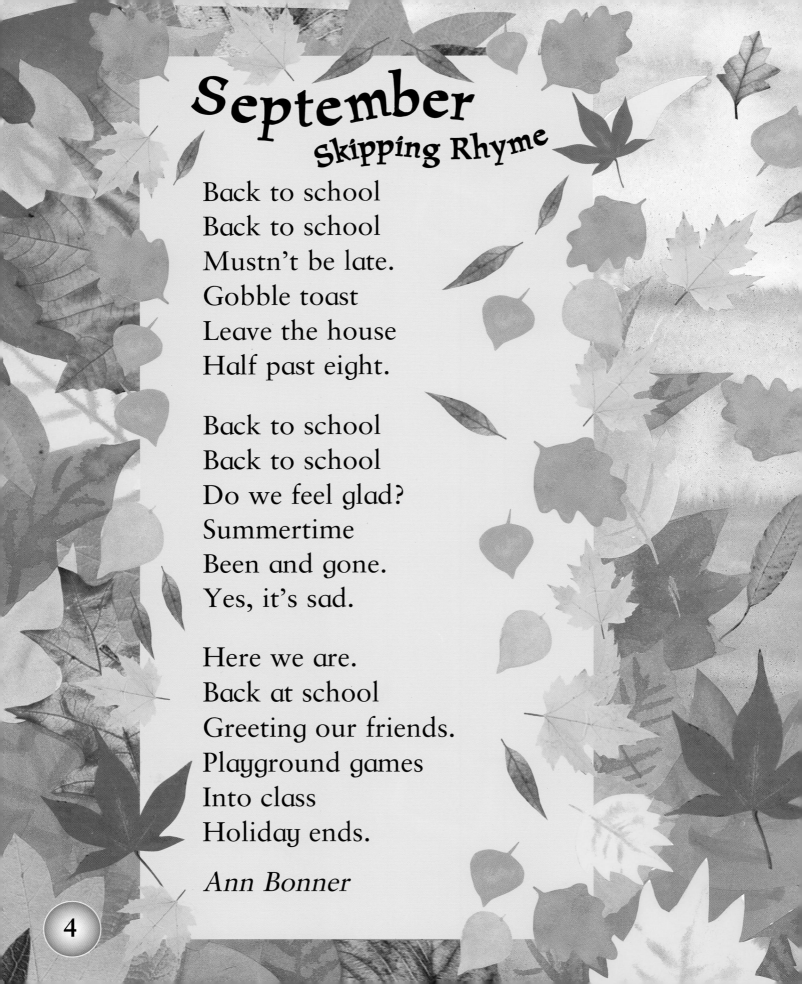

September

Skipping Rhyme

Back to school
Back to school
Mustn't be late.
Gobble toast
Leave the house
Half past eight.

Back to school
Back to school
Do we feel glad?
Summertime
Been and gone.
Yes, it's sad.

Here we are.
Back at school
Greeting our friends.
Playground games
Into class
Holiday ends.

Ann Bonner

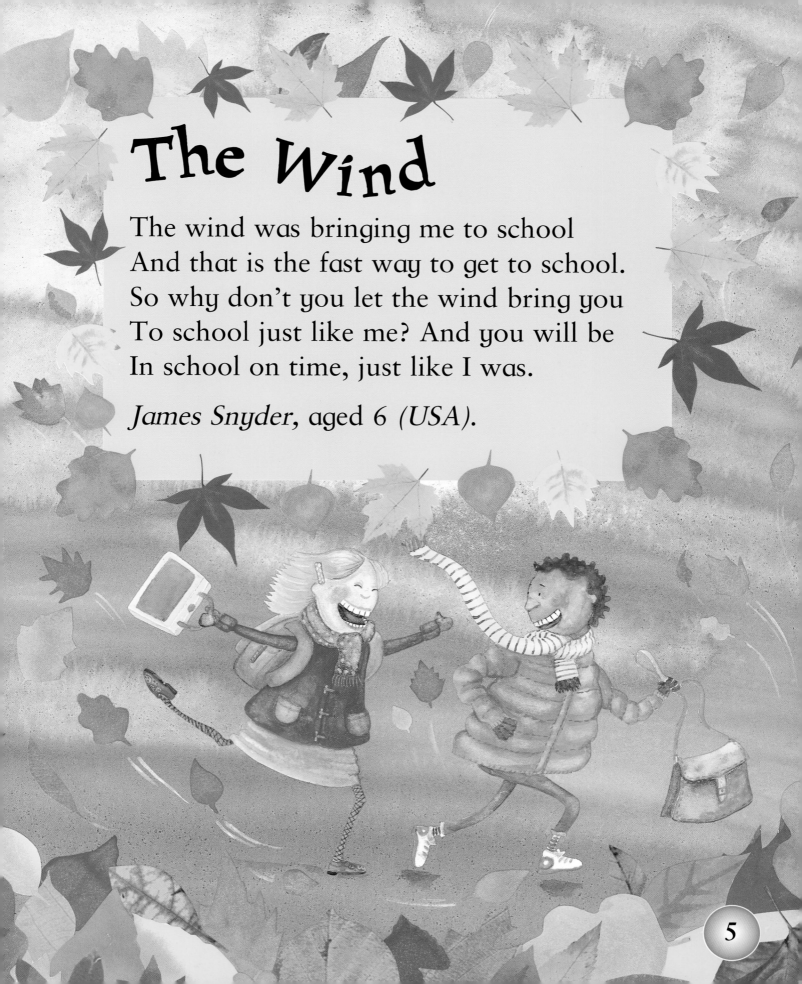

The Wind

The wind was bringing me to school
And that is the fast way to get to school.
So why don't you let the wind bring you
To school just like me? And you will be
In school on time, just like I was.

James Snyder, aged 6 *(USA)*.

Another Day

Boys shout,
Girls giggle,
Pencils write,
Squiggle squiggle.
Get it wrong,
Cross it out,
Bell's gone!
All out!

Balls bounce,
Hands clap,
Skipping ropes,
Slap slap.
Hand-stands,
By the wall,
Sara Williams
Best of all.
Boys fight,
Girls flee,
Teacher's gone
And spilt
His tea!

Clatter bang!
Big din!
Whistle goes,
All in!

All quiet,
No sound,
Hear worms,
Under ground.
Chalk squeaks,
Clock creeps,
Head on desk,
Boy sleeps.

Home time!
Glory be!
Mum's got
Chips for tea.
Warm fire,
Full belly,
Sit down,
Watch telly.

Bed time,
Creep away,
Dream until,
Another day.

John Cunliffe

Pufiki

There is a little boy.
His name is Jon.
When you say, "Go to school,"
He refuses utterly.
Says he "I will stay home
To cut fruit from the palm tree."
Pufiki! Pufiki! His name is Jon.
Pufiki! Pufiki! His name is Jon.

Anonymous (Nigeria)

New Boy

Today
everyone is laughing
at your long name
and your skinny legs
which look like
two burnt out matches
but by next week
I bet
they'll be your friends.

Pauline Stewart
(Caribbean)

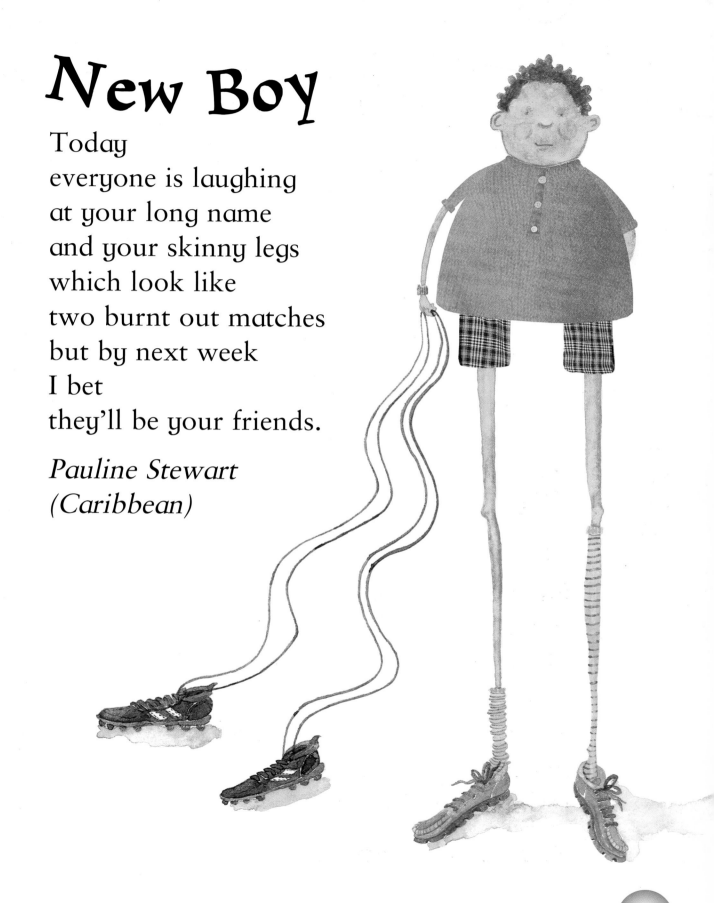

Do You Know my Teacher?

She's got a piercing stare
and long black . . .

(a) moustache
(b) hair
(c) teeth
(d) shoes

She eats chips and beef
and has short sharp . . .

(a) nails
(b) fangs
(c) doorstoppers
(d) teef

She is slinky and thin
and has a pointed . . .

(a) banana
(b) chin
(c) beard
(d) umbrella

She has a long straight nose
and hairy little . . .

(a) kneecaps
(b) ears
(c) children
(d) toes

She has sparkling eyes
and wears school . . .

(a) dinners
(b) trousers
(c) ties
(d) buses

She comes from down south
and has a very big . . .

(a) vocabulary
(b) handbag
(c) bottom
(d) mouth

She yells like a preacher
yes, that's my . . .

(a) budgie
(b) stick
(c) padlock
(d) teacher!

John Rice

Learning to Write

Learning to write with a leaky pen.
It's no fun.
I keep trying again,
And again,
And again,
But it's no use.
Every time
I do my best
But it always goes

Drip!

Drop!

Trickle!

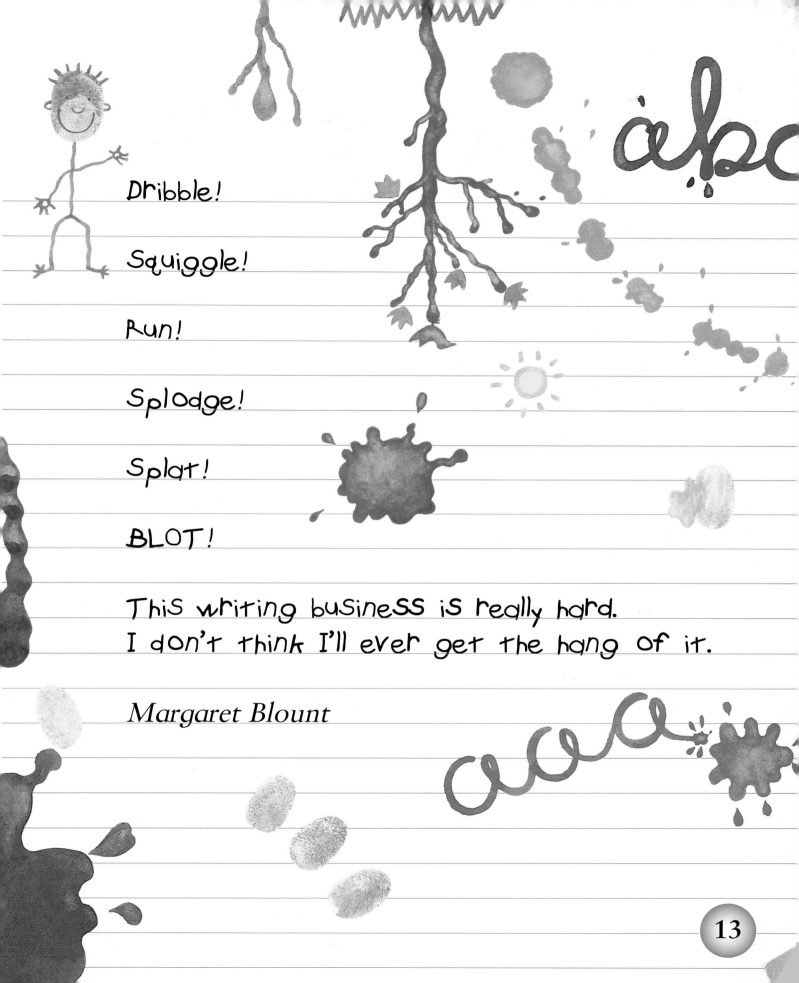

Dribble!

Squiggle!

Run!

Splodge!

Splat!

BLOT!

This writing business is really hard.
I don't think I'll ever get the hang of it.

Margaret Blount

On the Playground

Children bumping,
children thumping,
children jumping, jumping, jumping.

Children creeping,
children weeping,
children leaping, leaping, leaping.

Children crashing,
children bashing,
children dashing, dashing, dashing.

Children hopping,
children flopping

(There goes the bell!)

Children. . . stopping.

Wes Magee

Playground Haiku

Everyone says our
playground is overcrowded
but I feel lonely.

Helen Dunmore

Hopscotch

A hip hop hippity hop
yes it's time to play hopscotch
hip hop hippity hop
yes it's time to play hopscotch

a turn and a twist
we make a double fist
a jump and a spin
we go right in

a flop and a hop
I spin like a top
Jessie now stands upside down
her smile looks just like a frown

Hey!
a hip hop hippity hop
me and my friends play hopscotch
jumping
   laughing
      running
screaming
hip
   hop
      hippity
hop

we are all having fun
wanting to play till the day is done
until Gloria the big bully
comes and yells

BOYS DON'T PLAY HOPSCOTCH!!!

Afua Cooper (Jamaica)

Classes under the Trees

My teacher, Mrs Zettie, says,
"Children, we can't breathe in here.
Come on! We're going
under the breadfruit tree!"

We leave the one room schoolhouse
these hot days in June
for the breeze outdoors
below blue skies.

Reciting our lessons
in singsong fashion,
we hear twittering birds
recite theirs, too.

Monica Gunning (Caribbean)

A Dragon in

There's a dragon in the classroom:
its body is a box,
its head's a plastic waste bin,
its eyes are broken clocks,

its legs are cardboard tubes,
its claws are toilet rolls,
its tongue's my dad's old tie
(that's why it's full of holes).

the Classroom

"Oh, what a lovely dragon,"
our teacher smiled and said.
"You <u>are</u> a pretty dragon,"
she laughed and stroked its head.

"Oh no, I'm not," he snorted,
SNAP! SNAP! he moved his jaw
and chased our screaming teacher
along the corridor.

Charles Thomson

Snake in School

One year in the Monsoon season
We all screamed and with good reason:
A water snake had come to school!
But Mister Singh just kept his cool.
He chased him out of our school gate
And told him off for being late!

Debjani Chatterjee (India)

Sometimes during storytimes

Timothy sucks his tie

Oliver chews his dinosaur rubber

Rosalyn goes cross-eyed

Yoshi eats her pony tail

Tabatha bites her vest

Isobel wiggles her ears round and round

Me? What do I like best?

Eating that bit of old bubble gum

Someone left under my desk

James Carter

Whiz Kid

Beth's the best at reading,
Gary's good at sums,
Kirsty's quick at counting
On her fingers and her thumbs,

Wayne's alright at writing,
Charles has lots of chums
But I'm the fastest out of school
When home time comes.

Gina Douthwaite

O.K. but . . .

School's O.K.,
You have some fun -
But school is better
When it's done!

Clive Webster

The Lollipop Lady

When
we come to the
busy street we stand
beside the kerb and wait.
The lady with the lollipop
makes the teatime traffic stop.
When it's our turn to go across
even the hugest lorries pause.
Her lolly's like a magic wand –
cars bicycles and buses stand
and wait until we're over on
the other pavement. Once
we've gone the traffic all
begins to flow
but only

when she signals GO!

Pamela Gillilan

Down by the School Gate

There goes the bell,
it's half-past three,
and down by the school gate
you will see. . .

Ten mums talk talk talking,
Nine babies squawk squawking,
Eight toddlers all squabbling,
Seven grans on bikes, wobbling. . .

Six dogs bark bark barking,
Five cars stopping, parking,
Four child-minders running,
Three bus drivers sunning. . .

Two teenagers dating,
One lollipop man, waiting. . .

The school is out,
it's half-past three,
and the first to the school gate
. . . is me!

Wes Magee

Nothing Special

I've got grass stains on my bottom
and paint marks on my shirt,
my pencil case took a walk,
I spilt milk down Nicola's shirt.

My jumper has gone at the sleeves
and there's Plasticine in my hair.
I've cracked a lens in my glasses,
my shoes are beyond repair.

I lost my towel after swimming
and someone has taken a sock.
I shut myself in the toilet
then I couldn't undo the lock.

Our teacher says a magician
must have been in our room last night,
several things have gone missing,
disappeared from sight.

That big lad in the juniors
called me a sad little fool.
No nothing special happened Mum,
just another normal day at school.

Brian Moses

Further Information

Following on from any reading of a poem, either individually or in groups, check with the children that they have understood what the poem is about. Ask them to point out any difficult words or lines and explain these. Ask children how they feel about the poem. Do they like it? Is there a particular section or line in the poem that they really enjoy?

The two poems by Wes Magee may promote a number of activities. Read 'On the Playground' and discuss whether this is an accurate picture of what happens on most playgrounds. Can children add appropriate actions as it is read – a large space such as the school hall may be useful here! Using this poem as a model, children may enjoy writing their own poems based on other times of day – a lesson in the gym or lunchtime:

> Children crunching,
> children scrunching,
> children munching, munching, munching.
>
> Teachers meeting,
> teachers greeting,
> teachers eating, eating, eating.

'Down by the school gate' by Wes Magee is a countdown poem that may also prove useful as a model for children's own writing. Again try different times of day. Another example of a countdown poem 'Through the Staffroom Door' may be found in *The Secret Lives of Teachers*. (See the book list).

Both 'Skipping Rhyme' by Ann Bonner and 'Another Day' by John Cunliffe use short lines of two or three words. Children may enjoy composing their own poems in this way.

Contrast the two short poems by Helen Dunmore and Pauline Stewart. Both consider how some children may be lonely at school. Encourage children to discuss the poems and to put forward ideas as to what can be done to help children who are lonely. Can they remember their first day at school. How did they feel?

Encourage children to look for further examples of poetry about school. These can be copied out and then illustrated. Build up a collection of poems and let children talk about their favourites. Let them practise reading and performing the poems adding actions and percussion accompaniment if appropriate.

Such activities as these will promote and reinforce the suggested work at various levels in the National Literacy Strategy.

About the Poets

Margaret Blount lives in Doncaster where she is the headteacher of a rural primary school. She began writing poetry to amuse her three daughters.

Ann Bonner lives in the West Midlands. She has been a teacher and writer for the last 35 years. She currently works as a writer in schools and a teacher of people with learning difficulties.

James Carter is a freelance teacher and writer who lives in Berkshire. He tutors courses on creative writing and children's literature at Reading University. His latest title, *Talking Books* (Routledge) is a series of interviews with children's authors.

Debjani Chatterjee was born in India but now lives in Sheffield. She frequently runs writing workshops and gives readings in the UK and abroad.

John Cunliffe lives in Yorkshire and has worked as a librarian, teacher, book-reviewer and TV presenter; for the past ten years he has also been a full-time writer. He is best known for his two television series, *Postman Pat* and *Rosie and Jim*, and has also had five works of poetry published.

Gina Douthwaite lives high on the Yorkshire Wolds where she writes poetry and stories for children. She also runs *Poetry Parties* in schools and a collection of shape poetry, *Picture a Poem* was published by Hutchinson in 1994.

Helen Dunmore writes fiction and poetry for children and adults, and has had more than twenty books published. Her latest children's novel is *Brother Brother, Sister Sister* (Scholastic).

Wes Magee was born in Greenock, Scotland and now lives in North Yorkshire. He is a former head teacher and has been a full time author since 1989. His most recent book is *The Phantom's Fang-tastic Show* (OUP).

Brian Moses lives on the coast in Sussex. He writes and edits books for children and travels the country performing his poems.

John Rice was born in Scotland and now lives in Kent. He tells stories and performs his poems for both children and adults throughout the country. In his spare time he runs marathons.

Charles Thomson lives in London and has been a full-time poet since 1987. He has visited over 700 schools and broadcast his poems on radio and television. His work is in over eighty anthologies.

Clive Webster is a retired English teacher who lives in Worksop. He has been writing verse – and worse – for over twenty years. He is a mad-keen sportsman.

Permissions

The compiler and publisher would like to thank the authors for allowing their poems to appear in this anthology. While every attempt has been made to gain permissions and provide an up-to-date biography, in some cases this has not been possible and we apologise for any omissions.

'Another Day' by John Cunliffe appears by kind permission of David Higham Associates; 'Classes under the Trees' by Monica Gunning from *Not a Copper Penny in Me House – Poems from the Caribbean*, is reproduced by kind permission of Macmillan Children's Books, London.

Books to Read

The following books may be useful to use alongside the poems featured in this collection:

Starting School by Janet & Allan Ahlberg (Puffin Picture Book, 1988). A delightful introduction to school life and a book that all young children should hear in their first term at school.

Lucy & Tom Go To School written and illustrated by Shirley Hughes (Picture Puffin, 1992). Another lovely book about two young children's first experiences of school life.

How to Write Really Badly by Anne Fine (Mammoth, 1996). Discover the 'Writer From Hell' and learn how he can be helped. A challenging read for the more capable reader.

Off to School – Poems for the Playground compiled by Tony Bradman (Macdonald Young Books, 1998). A lively collection of poems about many aspects of school life.

Please Mrs. Butler, verses by Allan Ahlberg (Puffin, 1984). A modern classic. Try 'Dog in the Playground' or the title poem. Children can't help but learn from these gems.

The Secret Lives of Teachers compiled by Brian Moses (Macmillan, 1996). Ever wondered what goes on behind the staffroom door, or what teachers do in their spare time – or even what they wear in bed?

Picture acknowledgements Hutchison Library 6-7; Wayland Picture Library 18-19.

Index of First Lines